LIBRA

SUN SIGN SERIES

LIBRA

SUN SIGN SERIES
JOANNA MARTINE WOOLFOLK

TAYLOR TRADE PUBLISHING
LANHAM • NEW YORK • BOULDER • TORONTO • PLYMOUTH, UK

Published by Taylor Trade Publishing
An imprint of The Rowman & Littlefield Publishing Group, Inc.
4501 Forbes Boulevard, Suite 200, Lanham, Maryland 20706
www.rlpgtrade.com

Estover Road, Plymouth PL6 7PY, United Kingdom

Distributed by National Book Network

British Library Cataloguing in Publication Information Available

Library of Congress Cataloging-in-Publication Data

Woolfolk, Joanna Martine.
  Libra / Joanna Martine Woolfolk.
    p. cm.—(Sun sign series)
  ISBN 978-1-58979-559-4 (pbk. : alk. paper)—ISBN 978-1-58979-534-1 (electronic)
  1. Libra (Astrology) I. Title.
  BF1727.45.W66 2011
  133.5'272—dc22   2011003084

∞™ The paper used in this publication meets the minimum requirements of American
National Standard for Information Sciences—Permanence of Paper for Printed Library
Materials, ANSI/NISO Z39.48-1992.

Printed in the United States of America

I dedicate this book to the memory of
William Woolfolk
whose wisdom continues to guide me,

and to
James Sgandurra
who made everything bloom again.

CONTENTS

ABOUT THE AUTHOR

Astrologer Joanna Martine Woolfolk has had a long career as an author, columnist, lecturer, and counselor. She has written the monthly horoscope for numerous magazines in the United States, Europe, and Latin America—among them *Marie Claire*, *Harper's Bazaar*, *Redbook*, *Self*, *YM*, *House Beautiful*, and *StarScroll International*. In addition to the best-selling *The Only Astrology Book You'll Ever Need*, Joanna is the author of *Sexual Astrology*, which has sold over a million copies worldwide, and *Astrology Source*, an interactive CD-ROM.

Joanna is a popular television and radio personality who has been interviewed by Barbara Walters, Regis Philbin, and Sally Jessy Raphael. She has appeared in a regular astrology segment on *New York Today* on NBC-TV and on *The Fairfield Exchange* on

CT Cable Channel 12, and she appears frequently on television and radio shows around the country. You can visit her website at www.joannamartinewoolfolk.com.

ACKNOWLEDGMENTS

Many people contribute to the creation of a book, some with ideas and editorial suggestions, and some unknowingly through their caring and love.

Among those who must know how much they helped is Jed Lyons, the elegant, erudite president of my publishers, the Rowman & Littlefield Publishing Group. Jed gave me the idea for this Sun Sign series, and I am grateful for his faith and encouragement.

Enormous gratitude also to Michael K. Dorr, my literary agent and dear friend, who has believed in me since we first met and continues to be my champion. I thank Michael for his sharp editor's eye and imbuing me with confidence.

Two people who don't know how much they give are my beloved sister and brother, Patricia G. Reynhout and Dr. John T. Galdamez. They sustain me with their unfailing devotion and support.

*We are born at a given moment, in a given place,
and like vintage years of wine, we have the
qualities of the year and of the season
in which we are born.*

CARL GUSTAV JUNG

INTRODUCTION

When my publishers suggested I write a book devoted solely to Libra, I was thrilled. I've long wanted to concentrate exclusively on your wonderful sign. You are very special in the zodiac. Astrology teaches that Libra is the sign of partnership. Your sign represents harmony and loving relationships, elegance, an eye for beauty, creative talent, and star presence. You're gifted, gracious, and able to create balance—in art, your environment, and especially between people. Karmic teachers say you were specially picked to be a Libra because you were a great peacemaker in a previous life. But whether or not one believes in past lives, in *this* life you are Libra, the radiant, romantic spirit of cooperation and mutual accord.

These days it has become fashionable to be a bit dismissive of Sun signs (the sign that the Sun was in at the time of your birth). Some people sniff that "everyone knows about Sun signs." They say the descriptions are too cookie-cutter, too much a cardboard figure, too inclusive (how can every Libra be the same?).

Of course every Libra is not the same! And many of these differences not only are genetic and environmental, but are differences in your *charts*. Another Libra would not necessarily have your Moon sign, or Venus sign, or Ascendant. However, these are factors to consider later—after you have studied your Sun sign. (In *The Only Astrology Book You'll Ever Need*, I cover in depth differences in charts: different Planets, Houses, Ascendants, etc.)

First and foremost, you are a Libran. Libra is the sign the Sun was traveling through at the time of your birth.* The Sun is our most powerful planet. (In astrological terms, the Sun is referred to as a planet even though technically it is a "luminary.") It gives us life, warmth, energy, food. It is the force that sustains us on Earth. The Sun is also the most important and pervasive influence in your horoscope and in many ways determines how others see you. Your Sun sign governs your individuality, your distinctive style, and your drive to fulfill your goals.

Your sign of Libra symbolizes the role you are given to play in this life. It's as if at the moment of your birth you were pushed onstage into a drama called *This Is My Life*. In this drama, you are the starring actor—and Libra is the character you play. What aspects of this character are you going to project? The Libran intelligence, refinement, and social polish? Its communicative charm and artistic style, its amazing ability to create harmony in relationships? Or its difficulty making decisions, dependence on others, superficiality, avoidance tendencies? Your sign of Libra describes your journey through this life, for it is your task to evolve into a perfect Libran.

For each of us, the most interesting, most gripping subject is *self*. The longer I am an astrologer—which at this point is half my lifetime—the more I realize that what we all want to know about is ourselves. "Who am I?" you ask. You want to know what makes

*From our viewpoint here on Earth, the Sun travels around the Earth once each year. Within the space of that year, the Sun moves through all twelve signs of the zodiac, spending approximately one month in each sign.

you tick, why you have such intense feelings, and whether others are also insecure. People ask me questions like, "What kind of man should I look for?" "Why am I discontented with my job?" or "The man I'm dating is a Scorpio; will we be happy together?" They ask me if they'll ever find true love and when they will get out of a period of sadness or fear or the heavy burden of problems. They ask about their path in life and how they can find more fulfillment.

So I continue to see that the reason astrology exists is to answer questions about you. Basically, it's all about *you*. Astrology has been described as a stairway leading into your deeper self. It holds out the promise that you do not have to pass through life reacting blindly to experience, that you can within limits direct your own destiny and in the process reach a truer self-understanding.

Astrologically, the place to begin the study of yourself is your Sun sign. In this book, you'll read about your many positive qualities as well as your Libra issues and negative inclinations. You'll find insights into your power and potentials, advice about love and sex, career guidance, health and diet tips, and information about myriads of objects, places, concepts, and things to which Libra is attached. You'll also find topics not usually included in other astrology books—such as how Libra fits in with Chinese astrology and with numerology.

Come with me on this exploration of the "infinite variety" (in Shakespeare's phrase) of being a Libra.

Joanna Martine Woolfolk
Stamford, Connecticut
June 2011

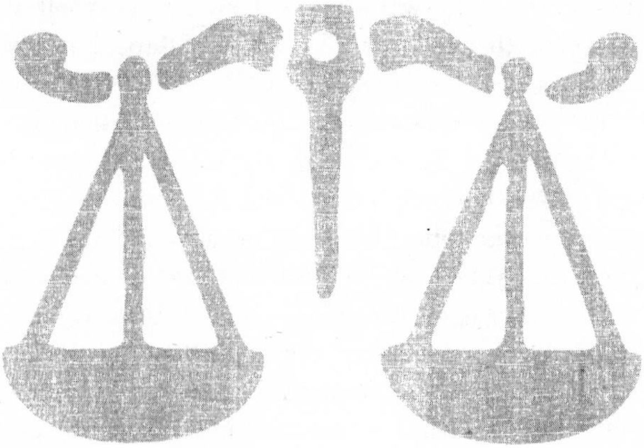

LIBRA

SEPTEMBER 22–OCTOBER 22

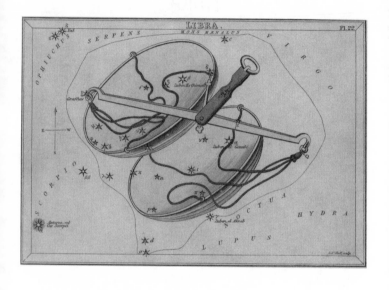

LIBRA.

MONS MÆNALUS

Pl. 22.

OPHIUCHUS   SERPENS   VIRGO

Yed

Graffias

Zuben Es Chinali

E   W

S

Zuben-el-Genubi

SCORPIO

Antares, vel
Cor Scorpii

Zuben-el-Akrab

NOCTUA   HYDRA

LUPUS

Sid. J. Hall Sculp.

PART ONE

ALL ABOUT YOU

ILLUMINATING QUOTATIONS

"I have the simplest tastes. I am always satisfied with the best."

—Oscar Wilde, writer, poet, and aesthete, a Libra

"I am a spy in the house of me. I report back from the front lines of the battle that is me."

—Carrie Fisher, actress and writer, a Libra

"Everything in life has to have balance."

—Donna Karan, fashion designer, a Libra

"Happiness is when what you think, what you say, and what you do are in harmony."

—Mohandas Gandhi, political and spiritual leader, a Libra

"Unless you love someone, nothing else makes any sense."

—e. e. cummings, poet, a Libra

"All you need is love."

—John Lennon, musician and member of the Beatles, a Libra

YOUR LIBRA PERSONALITY

YOUR MOST LIKEABLE TRAIT: Charm

The bright side of Libra: Adaptable, creative, romantic, good-natured, diplomatic, the peacemaker

The dark side of Libra: Indecisive, self-indulgent, dependent, frivolous, changeable, poor sense of self

Libra is the sign of partnerships and relationships, and you are gifted at blending with people. You feel incomplete when you're not part of others. An insidious side to this is Libra feels weak on its own and must discover (sometimes painfully) its inborn strength. Certainly, you're outgoing and communicative, and at your most radiant in social settings. Creating a pleasing environment is paramount; you have artistic imagination and refined sensibilities. You can also be vain and self-centered, and you greedily seek attention and flattery to prevent your shaky confidence from sagging. Libra's famous indecisiveness stems from always seeing two sides (at least) to every question and your anxiety about making a wrong decision.

You are very easy to like, for you have a captivating allure, possess elegant taste, and are usually beautiful to look at. In addition, you have the treasured gift of making others feel exciting and important. You're a superb listener and instinctively know how to draw out another person. Known for your velvet touch, you're famous for how effortlessly you smooth ruffled feathers, bring out smiles, and make others think they're the most wonderful person in the world. Your natural element is social life, parties, and entertainments where you magnetize others with your radiant graciousness. You're a born charmer.

Libra is the zodiacal sign of partnerships—in psychological terms, the sign is outer-directed. Your energies are focused on melding and combining with people. Whether they be partners, lovers, mates, family, friends, business associates, or even guests at your party—relationships are your métier. In the professional world, you're a superb team player. You're able to blend many disparate egos into one smooth-working union. Your friendships and associations bring opportunities, and your best luck comes when you pool your creative talents and intelligence with powerful individuals who open doors for you. You're simply not a loner.

Indeed, your arresting charm is rooted in your deep need for shared experience—the fact that you're a *sharer* is an important reason you're such a success with people. Whether with friends, business partners, lovers, or family, everything in your life is enhanced when you can share it. You don't sit alone and silent, pondering your triumphs and defeats. You open yourself to others, and in so doing you create a genuine bond.

However, you're a narcissist at heart, and your main interest is on yourself within the relationship. It's true you have superb intuitions in dealing with other people's emotions, and no one is better at understanding and taking into consideration another person's point of view. Yet all too soon that outside viewpoint will be lost or subsumed within your own subtly self-centered concerns. Your goal is to enchant others and be the jewel in the center of any setting. You want admiration, and you have a computer memory for any compliment ever paid to you. You tend to judge others by outward appearances; if someone has a charming façade, you won't look any deeper. As a result, you may become easy prey for a sophisticated schemer with an affable manner.

Ruled by Venus, Goddess of Love and Beauty, you're addicted to the beautiful side of life. You admire loveliness in all its forms, in music, art, decoration, and people. Your home will always have a touch of elegance, and you love to entertain in style. Flowers, champagne, lovely jewelry and clothes, beautiful (and expensive) *objets*, luxurious surroundings—these are the ornaments of life to you. You enjoy all the things that money can buy.

Born under the sign of the Scales, you crave balance, harmony, and being in equilibrium. You're happiest when your environment is ordered and serene, and you gloss over anything unrefined, mean, or ugly. You want life to be like a glamorous movie filled with beautiful people, music, romance, and a happy ending. Rose-colored glasses are your most important accessory.

Tact, diplomacy, and the art of cooperation are as natural to you as breathing—and because you see clearly every side of an argument, every possibility of a given course, you have the ability to smooth over disputes. In order to avoid an unpleasant scene, you will stifle your own true feelings. In fact, far too often you are not sure what your true feelings are. You try to be all things to all people, and therefore the general impression is you are indecisive. You appear constantly poised on an edge, seemingly unable to move one way or another, balancing pro with con, advantage with disadvantage, risk with gain. You're fond of saying, "On the one hand, but still, on the other hand. . . ." Underneath your genial, calm surface, you have to struggle in order to make decisions.

You'll also go a long way out of your way to avoid friction and dissension—peace is worth any price to you. And the issue of nonconfrontation goes even deeper: You're unable to speak up for yourself. You're a victim of accommodation. Of course, there comes a point when you do stand up for yourself, and usually this is over fair play. Librans have a reputation for stubbornness, yet this is because you are sticklers for fairness. You can become aggressive in situations in which you or someone else is getting the short end of the stick. In general, your strength is brought out by crisis; this is when you're at your most daring. Too often, though, on these occasions you're strident and off-putting, and you pick the inappropriate moment. It's hard to be clear and strong about oneself only infrequently. One must keep in practice.

The basic problem, Libra, is that you feel weak and incomplete in *yourself*. Beneath your brilliance and charm, you feel a psychic lack, something missing—whether this something is a perfect lover, a fulfilling career, a wonderful project that shows off your talents, or something else. You spend a lot of time feeling you're not "real," that you've conned others into thinking you're clever and successful. You're anxious about failing to live up to a glamorous and smart image. You worry that others aren't seeing you as the scintillating, spectacularly talented person you want them to see. You're careful not to make mistakes. To be humiliated or commit a social gaffe is horrifying and makes you feel others will now see you as a fraud. One of Libra's best-hidden secrets is how shaky your self-confidence is—and certainly your sense of not being whole and creating a false front is at the core of your insecurity.

You are a system of contradictions. You are kind, yet you have an indefinable aloofness, a detachment. You are openhearted but can close yourself off from others. At the same time that you're loving and attentive, it doesn't take much for your caring to evaporate as you sink back into self-absorption. You're very fragile, but also tough. You're generous, creative, humorous, and a blithe spirit, yet you can also be selfish, defensive, cynical, and frightened about your own security.

Of course, being human, each of us is a paradox, bursting with inconsistency. But for Libra, the issue is you look to others (particularly those you perceive as dominant) to validate you and provide a strong center. And, not surprisingly, this makes you angry, which you successfully keep hidden.

You do get along harmoniously with people who are easygoing and even-tempered, particularly those who can laugh in the face of difficulties. You are especially appreciative of talent in any field, whether art, literature, or music, and even if you lack talent yourself, you indulge in artistic hobbies. Often people are surprised at the wide range of your interests because you hide your superior intellect under an agreeable exterior.

Yet beneath your graceful exterior lurks the brain of a calculator. Others sometimes fail to see how smart you are because they look only at your surface attractions. You're a superb organizer and have a true politician's knack for recruiting the best talent to get the job done. Also, Libra is a Cardinal sign, which means you're an initiator. You love new projects, unusual people, and different ideas, and you'll travel anywhere. Gifted with imagination, flair, and *enthusiasm*, you have an open, independent mind that tries to evaluate the world dispassionately and rationally. You're a quick learner and have wonderful money-making instincts. You also have lavish money-*spending* instincts—your great weakness is a love of luxury. Indeed, money has a way of slipping through your fingers because it isn't money you love, it is the things money can buy.

A love for beauty leads many Librans to careers in art, decorating, the theater, and composing, but the approach often remains that of a dilettante who enjoys the reward but avoids the effort needed to attain it. People born under this sign tend to dislike hard work, and certainly a distaste for confrontation and conflict leads to being underachievers.

Though it's hard to categorize you, basically you're an incorrigible idealist and quintessential romantic. One of your nicest traits is your optimism. You fantasize happy tomorrows and look forward to living them. Cheerful, warmhearted, affectionate, sentimental, you do everything in your power to please. Your stock in trade is charm.

THE INNER YOU

You work hard trying to please others, and as a result, they find you captivating. However, beneath your friendly exterior, you desperately long for love and approval. You have trouble saying no to others' requests, and you take on too many jobs or commitments—and then to prove how nice you are, you keep smiling through the strain while you hide a lot of resentment. It might be more useful to spend time building up your self-esteem rather than looking to others to provide it for you. Basically, you give away your power. You hate anything unpleasant and avoid conflict, vulgarity, or strife. If life were a play, you'd always insist on a happy ending. The problem with trying to have constant peace and harmony is that you have trouble making decisions. At times you fear that any move you make will bring something terrible crashing down around you. If you could just lighten up and not be so hard on yourself, you'd be much more satisfied with what you do achieve. You have every ingredient for happiness!

HOW OTHERS SEE YOU

People feel important when they're with you because you always seem to understand their point of view. You are considered warm and outgoing because you know how to draw out people, and you're thought of as someone with an unparalleled ability to deal with the public. However, because you want others' approval, you tend to go along with what they want—and this sometimes makes you look wimpy. To some people, you also appear vain and overly concerned with your appearance. And your fondness for parties and social life gives the impression you're frivolous.

GUARD AGAINST: Becoming the Passive, Lazy Libra Who Wastes Yourself

The dark side of Libra is the one who looks for the easy way out, who manipulates others into taking care of you. In your life you want beauty, luxury, harmony, and lots of friendship, but when this inclination tips off-balance, you're prone to excess (e.g., too much partying and drinking, keeping late hours, undisciplined health habits, extravagant spending you can't afford). You are self-indulgent. You run away from the unpleasant—hard work, conflict, taking responsibility—and allow strong-minded others to make your decisions. It's so much easier if someone else does the planning, pays the bills, keeps you in the things that feed your cravings. It's so much more fun to play and travel and buy pretty luxuries than deal with the problems of real life. It's so comforting and supportive to feel admired by a wide social circle of people who think you're wonderful.

Balance is not something you are born with, but something you must learn. Being Libra means that you, more than others, must learn how quickly your scales can swing wildly off-kilter into excess, self-indulgence, passivity, and dependency. The major problem with giving in to the easy way is that you lose your power of control. You allow others to take you over, and you let all that Libran brilliance, talent, and genius slip away. However, when you can tap into your inborn Libran strength to be responsible for yourself, you will no longer be tempted to take the path of least resistance. When you are in Libran equilibrium—in balance—you will truly utilize your incomparable Libran gifts.

YOUR GREATEST CHALLENGE:
To Develop a Strong Sense of Self

For all your brilliance, charm, and star quality, you have difficulty cultivating a secure identity. Libra is the sign of partnership, and you naturally gravitate toward becoming part of a union. You're comfortable in relationships. You do not feel complete without an "other." Your other-oriented tendencies, added to a shaky sense of self, create a personality who can become very dependent.

Your inborn talent is to be a people-pleaser—to pass out compliments, be gracious, be accommodating. And Libra's habit of bending to others and allowing them to take the lead is an effective way of gaining approval. Not only do you lack confidence, you also have an ambivalent streak. Often you don't know what you really think. "Yes, I do feel this way, but still, on the other hand, I could be persuaded to go in another direction." Taken to extremes, your indecisiveness is an evasion of accountability and adapting to others a method of avoiding criticism and rejection.

It's a great challenge to be strong about self when the self feels weak. Yet your life lesson is to not give away your power and to see the psychological damage you do to yourself when you don't speak up and let others run your life. Astrology teaches that Libra is a glorious sign to be—just to start with you are highly intelligent, talented, imaginative, and alluringly attractive. And when you build your self-esteem, truly find your strong *self*, you can enter relationships as an equal. Then you will do the powerful creating you were born to do.

YOUR ALTER EGO

Astrology gives us many tools in our lives to help manage our struggles and solve problems. One of these tools is to reach into your opposite sign in the zodiac—your polarity. For you, Libra, this is Aries, sign of action, courage, and competition. Aries people thrive on challenge; they pull away from the "pack" and seek to differentiate themselves from others. Conversely, Libra is drawn toward integrating with others. Libra seeks identity within a relationship, although in fact far more often Libra loses (rather than finds) itself in a relationship. Unlike Aries, whose drive is to express its personality and rush ahead to seize all the prizes, you tend to look to others for validation. This may not be at all apparent—on the outside, you're vibrant, magnetic, and scintillating—but certainly the struggle to find approval and affirmation is a painful war within yourself. You're reluctant to risk rejection and do the hard emotional work of stepping up and out as an individual. The sad part of Libra is you never appreciate your splendid gifts as much as others do.

By tapping into Aries's boldness, its willingness to take risks, you can access the truly courageous part of yourself. Aries has an ability to say yes instead of no. You, too, possess this, but you closet it up inside you. It's safer to wrap yourself into another person you perceive as stronger than you and be taken care of. Yes, it's safer, but the price to pay is huge: your selfhood. You say to yourself, "I'm not brave enough," yet you really are. Even if you just *pretend* to be daring, you'll discover how powerful it feels to stand alone. You're extremely talented, smart, ambitious, and you're a fast learner. And by assuming some of Aries's attitude of "who cares what others think," you latch onto your own ability to set the world on fire. Aries has a heedless quality that can serve you well. Not that you would ever truly be heedless, but that impetuous capacity to say yes can zoom you past hesitation and, especially, past worrying you're not strong enough on your own.

In turn, Aries can learn much-needed lessons from you in how to include others, form meaningful and lasting bonds, be in give-and-take balance, and not barrel through life always thinking of "me first." Aries can use your graciousness and gift for understanding what others are feeling. And certainly Aries would make fewer missteps and mistakes by taking on some of your cautious approach to decision-making.

LIBRA IN LOVE

You could write the book on love—or at least on seduction. As a Libran, you are a true child of Venus, in love with the idea of being loved. The word *idea* is key. Libra is an Air sign, and, to you, love is an idea in your head more than an emotion in your heart. You're far less emotional than you are *romantic*. You live in your imagination and adore spinning romantic fantasies. Starting at a young age and down through the years, you carry within you the deep need for fantasy in your romantic life.

Pleasing others is a high priority, never more so than in a romantic relationship. Expert in the art of enchanting, you view seduction as an art form, and it's very easy to fall under your spell. You are, first and foremost, an actor, and your lovemaking is high drama, even though there is only an audience of one.

You are the sole person on stage. The spotlight is on you. In many ways, the signs of Libra and Leo share this star quality. But Leo likes to star on a bare stage with no accompaniment—and no distracting elements—whereas Libra is the glowing center of a special and rarified nimbus you create around you. To you the setting is important. Libra wants to be the brightest star in the heavens; Leo wants to be the Sun and fill the heavens with solitary splendor.

Your allure involves all the senses, for you're a creative artist. You know about food and wine, have refined taste in dressing and decoration, and are supremely talented in accentuating beauty and elegance. Of course you bring these aesthetic skills to sexual relationships. More than anyone else in the zodiac, you strive to create an ambiance of magic—candlelight, champagne, a luxurious setting. You use romantic touches (such as tucking little love notes in your lover's pocket or a tiny gift under his or her pillow) to make an affair sparkle.

The secret of your seductive charm is that you can tune into the moods and needs of a lover. You're exquisitely aware of nuance and subtle shifts in how your lover is reacting to you. Therefore, you're able to adjust to unspoken desires, weave a sensual spell, and create a storybook fantasy out of a real-life love affair.

If you're a Libran woman, you especially need to feel coddled and adored, and you crave all the trappings of romance (flowers, jewelry, surprise weekend getaways). This is why you tend to be attracted to older, richer men with experience in the art of pleasing a woman. In addition to affection, understanding, and sympathy, you want a lover who will cater to your whims. Being as adept as you are in reading unspoken messages, you also expect a lover to sense *your* desires without your having to declare them. A Libra woman usually attracts such men and often marries more than once.

Still, for all your mental smarts, emotionally you can be gullible and easily influenced. Particularly in your youth, your quest for love may lead you down different paths. In another era, you'd have fallen for the handsome card player working on a riverboat out of Natchez. But as time goes on, you become more discriminating. The glamour of transient affairs fades, and you are increasingly drawn to the luster of a permanent relationship.

If you're a Libran male, you're almost too popular with women because you have the rare ability to relate to them on what might be called a feminine level. You have great personal charm and a refined aesthetic sense. You get so much attention from the opposite sex that you're a little spoiled. If a woman doesn't catch your interest quickly, you tend to move to a more promising conquest. Practice has made you a suave lover. The real secret, though, to capturing your heart is to appeal to your *romanticism*.

You have a great flair for the dramatic: You will shower a woman with attention and presents, whisk the two of you off to exotic locales. But your lover cannot allow routine to set in or let herself become sloppy in appearance. You always need the illusion of romance—and you also need friendship and intellectual companionship.

For all Librans, love can be a complicated issue. Being gifted in the art of allure and enticement, and with your inborn talent for attracting others, you discover early on how to make others like you so that you receive the admiration you hunger for. A darker aspect to your ability to do this is that it can spill over into being manipulative—"I will give you my attention, affection, body, make you feel important and adored, if you will give me what I want." Libra is the sign of negotiating and bargaining, and in emotional terms, Libra's relationships have a close affinity to business mergers and striking a deal.

You do have a reputation of being a flirt, with a strong streak of fickleness. Yet it's less that you're faithless than that you're a natural-born charmer who loves attention. Also, you tend to pull away from a relationship when the emotional demands of the role become too much and you need a rest from the histrionics. Libra can be as lazy in love as in other areas. Besides, once you've satisfied your primary need—to enchant and dazzle—you begin losing interest.

However, when you truly fall in love with your whole heart, you are a faithful and committed partner. You put love on an idealized plane and tend to idolize your lover—and you're never more vibrant than when lavishing your abundant affections. For you, love is much more than physical passion. It is communion of spirit and intellect, shared goals, companionship, and genuine partnership.

TIPS FOR THOSE WHO WANT TO ATTRACT LIBRA

Librans are the jewels of the zodiac—the kind you see displayed in Tiffany's windows, not on Woolworth's shelves. They exist to be admired. Their milieu is that of the social arts, the world of good manners and pleasantries.

Don't fret about what topics to discuss. Librans have a great many interests—theater, music, antiques, decorating, art collecting—and are marvelous conversationalists. Of course, their favorite topic is themselves. You'll discover that even when they appear to be discussing something else, they're really talking about their own interests—in disguise. Pay the most generous compliment you can think of that has some grounding in truth and they'll be charmed by you.

If this becomes a bit wearing for you, switch to some controversial problem currently in the news. Take a strong position without being challenging or disagreeable. Librans are always interested in both sides of a question, and if you express a strong opinion, they will take pleasure in pointing out what's to be said for the other side. This won't lead to an argument or unpleasantness—Librans dread that—but might make for lively conversation. And if you tell Librans how smart they are and how much you've learned, you won't be making a mistake.

Librans dote on luxury and often judge people by the kind of places they go to. They believe first-class people never go to second-class places—unless they're slumming. Atmosphere means a good deal, and the wrong kind of setting is psychically disturbing. They don't care how expensive the right place is. Librans always think their pleasure is worth the price.

If you're trying to please a Libran, show that you have taste. Don't dress sloppily. Librans like to be proud of their dates. If you invite a Libran to your house, be sure the ambiance is right. No noisy sound-system, no garish lighting. Dinner had better be delicious (even if you order it sent up from an expensive restaurant) and served on your very best china and crystal—preferably by candlelight. Good music is always helpful. Librans respond to harmonious sounds.

In general, don't hold back on anything. Go all out. Whatever may be said against too much, too soon, Librans believe that's a lot better than too little, too late.

LIBRA'S EROGENOUS ZONES: Tips for Those with a Libra Lover

Our bodies are very sensitive to the touch of another human being. The special language of touching is understood on a level more basic than speech. Each sign is linked to certain zones and areas of the body that are especially receptive and can receive sexual messages through touch. Many books and manuals have been written about lovemaking, but few pay attention to the unique knowledge of erogenous zones supplied by astrology. You can use astrology to become a better, more sensitive lover.

If you want to get on more intimate terms with a Libra, try unobtrusively caressing his or her lower back when dancing or strolling together. The small of the back and the buttocks are very sensitive. When the relationship has progressed to the point where you are both in the bath or shower together, pay particular attention with a sponge or washcloth to Libra's lower back and buttocks. Gently sponge and lave this area with warm water until the skin is rosy.

Both male and female Librans are very partial to having their buttocks rubbed, fondled, patted, and gently pinched. An erotic massage technique that is sure to put a Libra into the mood for love is the following: (1) With Libra lying face-down, begin the massage by gently clutching one buttock in each hand and moving them in a circular motion. (2) With fingertips barely touching flesh, stroke the buttocks up and down with featherlight touches. (3) Do the same, using just fingernails. (4) Using four fingers of each hand, place your fingertips lightly on the buttocks, one finger at a time. Move quickly and lightly so that all the fingertips touch the skin in rapid succession. Position your hands so that the fingertips will land in the cleft between the buttocks.

By now Libra will be sexually aroused.

LIBRA'S AMOROUS COMBINATIONS: YOUR LOVE PARTNERS

LIBRA AND ARIES

Instantly, Aries falls under your sensual spell and you are captivated by Aries's dynamism. But while you two zodiacal opposites are immediately attracted to each other, tensions also immediately arise. Libra looks for harmony and peace, while restless Aries aggressively seeks new challenges and new worlds to conquer. For your taste, Aries is rude and tactless, whereas Aries thinks you are hopelessly unwilling to face facts. Aries is an attention-grabber, but you, who are secretly competitive, want people to focus on you. Aries needs to feel independent yet insists on unquestioning fidelity from its partner, and therefore can't forgive your indecisiveness about making a commitment. Passionate Aries is also offended by what it considers Libra's shallow emotions. Sexual rapport is wonderful for a while, but then what?

LIBRA AND TAURUS

The signs of Libra and Taurus are both Venus-ruled, and therefore you two would seem to have much in common. You do share a love of music and art, and you both have a deep need to be in a romantic bond. However, not much else pulls you together, and your personalities are poor fit. Taurus is a homebody, which bores you—you like to gad about and shine socially. You also adore spending money on luxuries, whereas Taurus advocates financial caution. You quickly lose patience with Taurus's stodgy attitudes and the fact that Taurus is so *un*-lighthearted. Worse, Taurus has a decidedly dictatorial streak, and much as you're willing to keep the peace, you simply won't be bossed. To boot, Taurus is jealous of your airy romantic nature. You two are sexually in tune, but when the song is ended, the malady lingers on.

LIBRA AND GEMINI

Pleasure-loving Libra and high-spirited Gemini are a fine mating. Both of you are lively, communicative Air signs who enjoy ideas, travel, spinning new plans, and keeping busy with a wide circle of friends. You two are curious, vivacious, and affectionate, and to you love is a carousel that never stops. True, the sexual fun and games are more frolicsome than deeply passionate, but neither of you cares as long as you're having fun. No jealousy or possessiveness will spoil your good times, although there can be trouble in paradise over Gemini's emotional detachment. Libra likes a shared life and to be in close harmony, and you take Gemini's airy aloofness as rejection. Also, you're both quite indecisive, so there'll be lots of discussion but not a lot of action. However, you both know how to use charm to get other people to do things for you.

LIBRA AND CANCER

At the beginning the sensuality level is high, for Cancer is passionate and emotional and wants to possess you. The problem is that Cancer is about owning and enclosing, and you want love to be a grand adventure with lots of luxury thrown in. It's doubtful that Cancer will ever understand Libra's romantic nature, and certainly Cancer is too cautious to press indecisive Libra for the response it needs. Very soon Cancer's clutching insecurity begins to feel suffocating. Disappointed at what it perceives as Libra's shallowness, Cancer turns sharply critical, and those crab-claws cut you deeply. Money-oriented Cancer is also annoyed by your extravagant tastes. You love the glittering social life; Cancer is happiest in the warmth of its own home. Problems might be solved in time, but the wait usually isn't worth it.

LIBRA AND LEO

Libra's amorous playfulness blends marvelously with Leo's dash and energy. You have magical sexual combustion because you both love to dramatize and be swept away. Leo's generous, expansive sensuality really lights your fire, and the thermometer moves up to torrid. Libra does have to approach Leo carefully on matters involving ego, but with your tact, that won't be a problem. In a real conflict, you know how to yield gracefully, and your sense of humor provides a light touch. Together, you're a creative, expressive super-couple who shares a love of luxury, going to parties where you're the center of attention, and creating a beautiful home that serves as a stage-set for you two stars. Over time, your friendship deepens—and this, bottom line, is what the two of you have together: a passionate friendship.

LIBRA AND VIRGO

At first you're drawn to Virgo's intelligence and discriminating taste, and together you have interesting conversations. But then compatibility comes to an abrupt end. Virgo takes love very seriously and has an analytical approach to how a relationship should develop. For Virgo, you're too affectionate and frivolous, and reserved Virgo doesn't know how to deal with this. And for you, Virgo is far too emotionally inhibited. Virgo won't express flowery admiration, which is the stuff of life to you. Stay-at-home Virgo resents your social butterfly instincts and pursuit of pleasure. Your tastes are expensive, but Virgo is careful, not to say miserly. You find Virgo fussy, nitpicking, critical, and completely inflexible. And Virgo's tendency to become dictatorial is the last straw. Love will have a short season for you two.

LIBRA AND LIBRA

Only a Libran truly understands another Libran, and the understanding between you is the glue that can hold you together. You'll need this, because your sameness is a major challenge. Both of you are equally demonstrative, lively, warm, sociable, and in love with beautiful things, and you enjoy pleasing each other in sexual ways. But there's a great sense of playing at love. A problem is that neither wants to face reality. Both of you are charming, peace-loving, and adaptable, but each needs a stronger balance than the other can provide. Also, each craves lots of attention, so you quickly become competitors. In addition, because you're so much alike, the specter of boredom lurks around the edges. Still, if each of you can find enough outside stimulation to whet your appetites, this can be an interesting liaison.

LIBRA AND SCORPIO

Immediately, Scorpio interests you because Libra adores interest-ing people. And Scorpio's intensity in love flatters you, who are always looking for any new form of attention. Indeed, Scorpio can plumb your erotic depths, bringing out facets to your sexuality you never knew you had. But Scorpio is also touchy, moody, and quick to lash out in anger, which is just the kind of person you cannot bear. Possessive Scorpio tries to control a lover, but you have a need for diversion and won't stay in Scorpio's net. Also, Scorpio is essentially a loner, which cuts you off from others. Your friendships and outside interests annoy Scorpio, and particularly your flirtatiousness and casual attitude toward sex completely in-furiate. As Scorpio seethes and becomes steadily more jealous and demanding, you have to either submit or leave.

LIBRA AND SAGITTARIUS

You want nothing more than an exciting, loving companion with whom to explore life, and Sagittarius fits the bill. You're stimulated by Sagittarius's expansive, adventurous outlook, and Sagittarius is drawn to your affectionate charm. Since you both gravitate to interesting people, good times, social life, and travel, you have much to fuel your relationship. Both of you are also both highly romantic, though this quality is more dominant in Libra. Sexually, Sagittarius is more physical and you are more imaginative. Also, you'll want to settle down before flighty Sagittarius does, but you can work this out. Charming, clever Libra knows how to appeal to Sagittarius's intellectual side, and you easily keep Sagittarius intrigued. Your pairing can develop into a fun-filled, free, delightful relationship.

LIBRA AND CAPRICORN

Capricorn is attracted to your style and all-around pizzazz—and you're intrigued by Capricorn's aura of stability and strength. Sexually, too, you have powerful chemistry, for Capricorn brings out your elegant eroticism. But for all Capricorn's physical intensity, he or she is guarded emotionally. You need flattery and attention, but Capricorn keeps its affections buried. Sentimental, in-love-with-love Libra won't get much understanding from realistic, materialistic Capricorn, and you feel cut off by Capricorn's remoteness. Also, Capricorn's autocratic manner exasperates you—while your playful, frivolous Libran ways offend Capricorn, who believes in hard work and achievement at any price. You're fond of socializing and nightlife, while Capricorn tends to be a loner, comfortable with only a chosen few. A short-lived romance.

LIBRA AND AQUARIUS

Your indolently sensual nature is stirred to life by Aquarius's bold and experimental lovemaking. Aquarius can arouse you in ways that are often a revelation. And you two have all the makings of a beautiful friendship: harmonious vibes in socializing, artistic interests, even an involvement in public affairs. You'll enjoy the friendship side of your affair as much as the romantic part. Indecisive Libra is delighted with the fact that quick-thinking Aquarius likes to make decisions. True, Aquarius can be quirky and a bit eccentric, but you have a laissez-faire tolerance for anyone with an original mind. You admire Aquarius's free spirit, and Aquarius adores your merry outlook. Each spurs on the other to live life as an adventure. With a satisfying love life and mutual enjoyment of living, all signals are go.

LIBRA AND PISCES

You start off fine, since both of you are sentimental, affectionate, and caring. What makes you most alike is the way you both want to impose your romantic visions on reality. Indeed, you are great romantics, full of fantasy, and together you two create an erotic love nest. But Pisces needs domination, reassurance, and constant attention, and you soon find that cloying and restrictive. The Libra personality is gregarious and fun-loving, but the more you're out and about, the more Pisces feels neglected and whines and scolds. Pisces thinks your commitment is insincere and your charm superficial. Ultimately, you see Pisces as weaker than you because Pisces cannot be the ballast you need to keep your ship on an even keel. Also, in the Libra-Pisces duo, Libra has to take the lead sexually, and you find that most annoying.

YOUR LIBRA CAREER PATH

You're the one with style and charm who brings people together and enters easily into relationships. You're the *harmonizing* communicator. Libra is the sign of partnership, and this is at the heart of the work you do best. You enjoy contact and find it second nature to cooperate and compromise. You're also supremely artistic and have an open, innovative mind. Therefore, the most successful professions for you are those that bring beauty into the world and in which you integrate with others (whether an audience, colleagues, communicating to the public in general, etc.). Your main concern—the thing you were born to do—is keep the harmony, and this applies to actual work (such as design) as well as to interpersonal relationships.

You dislike being alone, and a career that isolates you is not a good psychic fit. This doesn't mean you cannot create on your own (e.g., a writer who needs time and privacy to write his or her books or articles, or an entrepreneur who runs his or her own business). But overall you need to be part of a larger network of people with whom you interrelate.

You do reap the best results if you're linked to a strong partner or are part of a close-knit team with business skills. You're not especially hardheaded about practical concerns, although you appreciate financial security. (You tend to be a bit of a spendthrift, and enjoy feeling safe and coddled by money.) Yet for you, money is more a romantic fantasy than hard, cold cash, and your strong suit is never cutthroat negotiations. You do benefit from a more practical business partner.

Where you shine is in dealing with people. Caution, however: You are a people-pleaser and must guard against trying to make everyone happy. The saddest Libran is the one who stifles feelings and can't speak up—in fact, loses sight of his or her opinions. You'll quickly become miserable if you continually acquiesce to others in order to avoid unpleasantness. The optimum situation is to be in charge of a sphere that belongs completely to you and where your judgment takes precedence. This arrangement nurtures self-confidence and leaves little room for your insecurities to magnify.

Oddly, you yourself impose difficult-to-meet expectations on others, mainly having to do with acknowledgment of how valuable you are to them. You want warmth and appreciation (though you don't express this outright), and if you don't get this you become resentful. "See what I do for them," you fume to yourself, "and not a word of gratitude!"

A prime ingredient for happiness is to be emotionally involved in your work. It must have meaning for you—basically, your work has to bring more information, enlightenment, artistry, harmony, and cooperation to others.

With your aesthetic eye and superb taste, the world of the arts is open to you—you're drawn to anything to do with clothes, jewelry, cosmetics and hairdressing, crafts, design, or working with fabrics and color. This is a natural extension of your everyday interests.

You're also gifted in writing, drawing, photography, art, and architecture. You know how to please the public, so acting, modeling, lecturing, public relations, human resources, and sales work are other careers that suit your talents. The sign of Libra aligns with the concepts of justice and diplomacy; the legal profession and diplomatic service fit your innate skills.

The best working atmosphere is a tranquil one. You can't think straight if you're distracted by noise, tumult, messy surroundings, or (horrors) conflict.

You're surprisingly ambitious—surprising, that is, to other people, who see you as calm and laid back. Your ambition is not necessarily for fame (although this is lovely when it happens) but to *express* yourself. In many ways, Libra feels undefined (in your own mind's eye, you're a vague, indistinct image), but when you do a worthy job and put your own taste and expression into it, you are empowered. You become more "real." Becoming who you are is the essence of your ambition.

And as you go through this process, you must fight your tendency to put yourself down, feel "less than," feel you must be *perfect* or else you're not good enough. Many people have to overcome a lack of talent, but the only thing you have to overcome is lack of belief in yourself.

When you finally decide success is worth going after, here's what you must do: (1) Stop worrying about other people. It's truly not your job to keep everyone else happy. (2) Don't allow emotional problems in love, family, or relationships to interfere with your work. Try to keep them separate. (3) Practice self-discipline. Procrastination and mental laziness are your enemies. (4) Every day give yourself lots of praise for the things you do accomplish.

Your recipe for career fulfillment: Make sure you're connected to people who support and align with you—you come to life when you have others to relate to. Make sure your work expresses you (your opinions, judgments, taste, etc.). Make sure your work comes out of your heart's desire to bring what is harmonious and attractive into the world.

LIBRA AND HEALTH: ADVICE FROM ASTROLOGY

Libra has a complex, finely tuned system that requires balance in all respects (diet, exercise, sleep, recreation). You're susceptible to minor illnesses (such as colds), but your body's strong immunity quickly fights off germs, and you have huge bounce-back resilience. You have a tendency to gain weight easily, and you dislike exercise. Yet, again, the absolute key to optimum health is balance. Your metabolism works perfectly on a balanced diet of nutritious food— and not too much of it at one time. You have abundant energy but must use your energy steadily and evenly. You need regular, enjoyable exercise (no straining and exhaustion). And you must balance vigorous activity (such as hard work) with restorative sleep.

Advice and useful tips about health are among the most important kinds of information that astrology provides. Health and well-being are of paramount concern to human beings. Love, money, or career takes second place, for without good health we cannot enjoy anything in life.

Astrology and medicine have had a long marriage. Hippocrates (born around 460 B.C.), the Greek philosopher and physician who is considered the father of medicine, said, "A physician without a knowledge of astrology has no right to call himself a physician." Indeed, up until the eighteenth century, the study of astrology and its relationship to the body was very much a part of a doctor's training. When a patient became ill, a chart was immediately drawn up. This guided the doctor in both diagnosis and treatment, for the chart would tell when the crisis would come and what medicine would help. Of course, modern Western doctors no longer use astrology to treat illness. However, astrology can still be a useful tool in helping to understand and maintain our physical well-being.

THE PART OF YOUR BODY RULED BY LIBRA

Each sign of the zodiac governs a specific part of the body. These associations date back to the beginning of astrology. Curiously, the part of the body that a sign rules is in some ways the strongest and in other ways the weakest area for natives of that sign.

Your sign of Libra rules the kidneys, the lumbar region (which includes the lower spine and back), and the buttocks. Libra women tend to have graceful lower spines and curvaceous buttocks, and Libra men have well-shaped, muscular backs. Psychologically as well as physically, you have backbone (a strong constitution) and, as a rule, enjoy good health. Sometimes in adolescence your health is delicate, and then it balances out in adulthood.

Venus, the planet that rules Libra, holds sway over skin, hair, and veins, as well as the throat, kidneys, and lumbar region. You are known for your fine (though sensitive) skin, pleasing features, and good bone structure. When called on, your energy level can keep up with the best, although you are usually a slow starter in the morning.

Libra is prone toward weakness in the lower back, and this is the first place in the body to suffer when you overexert yourself. You're also predisposed toward kidney ailments and skin breakouts. In winter you may be afflicted with cold hands and feet because of poor circulation.

In many ways, your health is influenced by your surroundings and relationships. Any disturbance, dissension, or disagreement makes you wretchedly unhappy and undermines your ability to work or function.

DIET AND HEALTH TIPS FOR LIBRA

Balance is the key to Libra's health and well-being—balanced diet, balance of work and recreation, and balanced relationships with other people.

Libra's cell salt* is sodium phosphate, which equalizes the balance of acids and alkalis in the body and rids the body of waste material. It's important for you to keep a proper balance between acids and alkali in the body, for too much acidity will interfere with proper kidney function. The skin is a good indicator of whether more sodium phosphate is needed in the diet: Your skin tends to get yellowish and sallow when there is a deficiency. Good food sources for this mineral are strawberries, apples, raisins,

---

*Cell salts (also known as *tissue salts*) are mineral compounds found in human tissue cells. These minerals are the only substances our cells cannot produce by themselves. The life of cells is relatively short, and the creation of new cells depends on the presence of these minerals.

almonds, asparagus, peas, corn, carrots, spinach, beets, radishes, tomatoes, wheat, brown rice, and oatmeal. You function best with a balanced diet of protein and complex carbohydrates that is low in fat, sugar, and acid-producing foods. You should eat lots of broiled fish, seafood, and poultry (not too much beef or pork), low-fat cheeses, yogurt, plenty of fresh fruits and vegetables, salad greens, and whole-grain breads.

You were born with good looks but also with a tendency to gain weight. Fat will quickly detract from your appearance, and carrying around excess pounds is unhealthy. You definitely benefit from regular exercise to keep you fit in body and mind and to regulate your metabolism. The best exercises for Libra are graceful and aesthetic—for example, dancing, swimming, tai chi, yoga.

Your sensitive skin immediately shows the effect of lack of sleep, rich food, and too much champagne. You should drink plenty of pure water to keep your system flushed out and free of toxins, and you should avoid alcohol and carbonated drinks, which are bad for the kidneys. You should also use caution when trying new skin preparations, many of which cause your skin to break out. Back exercises will strengthen a weak lower back and keep your body supple. Good posture will free you from vague aches and pains in the back.

In general, try to surround yourself with beautiful things, pleasant music, and harmonious people. This is good advice for everyone, but emphatically important for you.

THE DECANATES AND CUSPS OF LIBRA

Decanate and *cusp* are astrological terms that subdivide your Sun sign. These subdivisions further define and emphasize certain qualities and character traits of your Sun sign, Libra.

WHAT IS A DECANATE?

Each astrological sign is divided into three parts, and each part is called a *decanate* or a *decan* (the terms are used interchangeably).

The word comes from the Greek word *dekanoi*, meaning "ten days apart." The Greeks took their word from the Egyptians, who divided their year into 360 days.* The Egyptian year had twelve months of thirty days each, and each month was further divided into three sections of ten days each. It was these ten-day sections the Greeks called *dekanoi*.

Astrology still divides the zodiac into decanates. There are twelve signs in the zodiac, and each sign is divided into three

*The Egyptians soon found out that a 360-day year was inaccurate and so added on five extra days. These were feast days and holidays, and not counted as real days.

decanates. You might picture each decanate as a room. You were born in the sign of Libra, which consists of three rooms (decanates). In which room of Libra were you born?

The zodiac is a 360-degree circle. Each decanate is ten degrees of that circle, or about ten days long, since the Sun moves through the zodiac at approximately the rate of one degree per day. (This is not exact because not all of our months contain thirty days.)

The decanate of a sign does not change the basic characteristics of that sign, but it does refine and individualize the sign's general characteristics. If you were born, say, in the second decanate of Libra, it does not change the fact you are Libran. It does indicate that you have somewhat different and special characteristics from those Librans born in the first decanate or the third decanate.

Finally, each decanate has a specific planetary ruler, sometimes called a subruler because it does not usurp the overall rulership of your sign. The subruler can only enhance and add to the distinct characteristics of your decanate. For example, your entire sign of Libra is ruled by Venus, but the second decanate of Libra is subruled by Uranus. The influence of Uranus, the subruler, combines with the overall authority of Venus to make the second decanate of Libra unlike any other in the zodiac.

FIRST DECANATE OF LIBRA

September 23 through October 2
Keyword: Magnetism
Constellation: Corvus, the Crow, symbolizing idealism and a sense of duty.
Planetary Subruler: Venus

Venus is both your ruler and subruler, which intensifies your Libran love for beauty, pleasure, and luxury. You tend to have extravagant tastes and often have trouble holding on to money. Blessed with great social charm, you strive to make an impact. To a large extent, the way you feel about yourself is determined by how much love you receive from others, and in general you try to achieve your goals through other people. Sometimes you cover up a lack of self-confidence by being the aggressor or the one who initiates projects. You have a creative nature that welcomes new ideas, and you are fond of travel. In love, you are romantic and impulsive, but you have a tendency to choose lovers who take more than they give.

SECOND DECANATE OF LIBRA

October 3 through October 13
Keyword: Endurance
Constellation: Centaurus, the Centaur, the magical half-man, half-horse who symbolizes duality in human beings.
Planetary Subruler: Uranus

Uranus, planet of the intellect, rules your decanate, giving power to the romantic qualities of Libra's Venus. The sharpness of your mind surprises people since your personality tends to be serene and charming. The Scales (Libra's symbol) also represent a duality that often makes you feel like two different people. There is a radiance to you, an artistic and original style, matched with a determination to accomplish what you set out to do. You are an independent person, yet you need companionship and love. Endurance and conservatism are hidden in your depths. You are at your best in social situations; this is where you come to life and shine.

THIRD DECANATE OF LIBRA

October 14 through October 22
Keyword: Order
Constellation: Corona Borealis, the Northern Crown, the bridal crown of Ariadne. Christian astronomers called it the Crown of Thorns. Corona Borealis symbolizes achievement.
Planetary Subruler: Mercury

The energy and quickness of Mercury join with Libra's Venus to give you an attention-getting personality. You have both vitality and likeableness, a combination that indicates success working with the public. Your mind is forceful, curious, open to new ideas. In general, you tend to follow your head rather than your heart. You enjoy sifting through information and making a reasonable and balanced judgment. Your pronounced intellectual capabilities are part of your allure; you have much sex appeal and enjoy attention from a wide range of people. Sometimes the depth of your true feeling for a lover is not apparent on the surface. Though you have a talent for the written word, you find it difficult to speak of your emotions.

WHAT IS A CUSP?

A cusp is the point at which a new astrological sign begins.* Thus, the cusp of Libra means the point at which Libra begins. (The word comes from the Latin word *cuspis*, meaning "point.")

When someone speaks of being "born on the cusp," that person is referring to a birth time at or near the beginning or the end of an astrological sign. For example, if you were born on October 22, you were born on the cusp of Scorpio, the sign that begins on October 23. Indeed, depending on what year you were born, your birth time might even be in the first degree of Scorpio. People born on the very day a sign begins or ends are often confused about what sign they really are—a confusion made more complicated by the fact that the Sun does not move into or out of a sign at *exactly* the same moment (or even day) each year. There are slight time differences from year to year. Therefore, if you are a Libran born on September 23 or October 22, you'll find great clarity consulting a computer-chart that tells you exactly where the Sun was at the very moment you were born.

As for what span of time constitutes being born on the cusp, the astrological community holds various opinions. Some astrologers claim cusp means being born only within the first two days or last two days of a sign (though many say this is too narrow a time frame). Others say it can be as much as within the first ten days or last ten days of a sign (which many say is too wide an interpretation). The consensus is that you were born on the cusp if your birthday is within the first *five* days or last *five* days of a sign.

*In a birth chart, a cusp is also the point at which an astrological House begins.

The question hanging over cusp-born people is "What sign am I really?" They feel they straddle the border of two different countries. To some extent, this is true. If you were born on the cusp, you're under the influence of both signs. However, much like being a traveler leaving one country and crossing into another, you must actually *be* in one country—you can't be in two countries at the same time. One sign is always a stronger influence, and that sign is almost invariably the sign that the Sun was actually in (in other words, your Sun sign). The reason I say "almost" is that in rare cases a chart may be so heavily weighted with planets in a certain sign that the person more keenly feels the influence of that specific sign.

For example, I have a client who was born in the evening on October 22. On that evening, the Sun was leaving Libra and entering Scorpio. At the moment of her birth, the Sun was still in Libra, so technically speaking she is a Libran. However, the Sun was only a couple hours away from being in Scorpio, and this person has the Moon, Mercury, and Venus all in Scorpio. She has always felt like a Scorpio and always behaved as a Scorpio.

This, obviously, is an unusual case. Generally, the Sun is the most powerful planetary influence in a chart. Even if you were born with the Sun on the very tip of the first or last degree of Libra, Libra is your Sun sign—and this is the sign you will most feel like.

Still, the influence of the approaching sign or of the sign just ending is present, and you will probably sense that mixture in yourself.

BORN SEPTEMBER 23 THROUGH SEPTEMBER 27

You are Libra with Virgo tendencies. You are people-oriented and possess a talent for making others like you. You are also industrious and have a keen eye for detail, but sometimes take on more than you can handle. It is important to you to be admired. You are aware of your public image and always strive to make the best impression. You would like to keep your emotions on an even keel, but you tend to be either enthusiastically happy or else dejected over some little thing going wrong. Love makes you feel fulfilled, and you are probably flirtatious.

BORN OCTOBER 18 THROUGH OCTOBER 22

You are Libra with Scorpio tendencies. You have magnetic personal charm and usually try to maneuver situations so you are the one who controls or directs. You know how to work hard, and you apply yourself wholeheartedly to achieve a goal. You are skillful in dealing with people. Your sensuality attracts others, even when you are not aware of it. At times you can be impatient and quick-tempered, but basically you don't like arguments and are willing to keep peace. You have a captivating social nature. Punctuality is not one of your strong points.

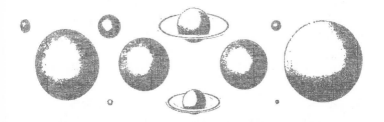

YOUR SPECIAL DAY OF BIRTH

SEPTEMBER 23

You're friendly, freedom-oriented, and like to talk about anything. People find you interesting because you're a born rebel with a far-out imagination. In love, you strive to be rational but are really an impulsive romantic not always smart about your choices.

SEPTEMBER 24

Being both restless and practical, and having a quick instinct for business opportunity, you'll achieve financial stability later in life. You also have a beguiling way with people. When you fall in love, you give your whole heart.

SEPTEMBER 25

You're both courageous and impatient, and you stand out from the ordinary. You have presence; people sense your personal strength and like to align themselves with you. You're an ardent romantic and a sexy lover who adores fantasy.

SEPTEMBER 26

The twinkle in your eye and your silver tongue make you an instant social hit. Yet you're also an intense go-getter with great expectations and the courage to pursue your goals. Romantically, you attract many, but you're picky and choose few.

SEPTEMBER 27

Your dynamic force keeps you a step ahead of others. You're a reluctant leader who would really like to be left alone to create independently. Love gives you the emotional grounding you seek, yet you're also flirtatious and need freedom.

SEPTEMBER 28

You're a precise thinker who's unpredictable emotionally, which makes you an artist at heart with an instinct for seeing where the profit lies. Love is turbulent and passionate, but ultimately you're destined to have a loyal, stable life-partner.

SEPTEMBER 29

You're an idealist and a lover of culture. With your sharp mind and voracious appetite for knowledge, you make a fine writer, historian, film buff. In romantic affairs, you give the impression of sophistication, but are really very vulnerable.

SEPTEMBER 30

Unlike many, you know who you are, and this provides a strong counterbalance to your ultrasympathetic heart. You're also funny, highly talkative, and on the move. When you fall in love, you give tenderness, devotion, and intense sexual passion.

OCTOBER 1

Outwardly, you're forceful and focused. Inwardly, you're sensitive and compassionate, filled with artistic imagination. In love, you look for a soulmate who will complete you, but relationships will always be a complicated mystery.

OCTOBER 2

People think you're ordered and conservative, but at heart you're a rebel. Basically, you live by your own high ethics and never follow the crowd. Romantically, you're at your best—supportive, reassuring, passionate, though you do tend to be a rescuer.

OCTOBER 3

You have a dynamic social side that draws many admirers, but you can also be a quiet hermit. You're a thinker and creator, and will carve out an unusual career. You want grand romance, yet relationships tend to fall short of what you long for.

OCTOBER 4

Rarely do you show self-doubt, even though you feel it, yet your inner courage keeps you strong. You're gifted intellectually and possess talents others envy. You've always been smart beyond your years—except in love, where you tend to choose needy partners.

OCTOBER 5

You charm others with your sharp wit and amusing eccentricities. They see a steamroller personality, though you're actually a softie at heart. You're impetuous in sexual affairs, but what you truly need are friendship and intellectual companionship.

OCTOBER 6

Compassionate love is central to your being. You're caring and deeply sensitive, and this extends to the way you perform in your career. You're a committed perfectionist. Your difficulty in intimacy is trying too hard to make the other person happy.

OCTOBER 7

Feelings drive you—though you're convinced you operate solely from your head—and you channel your emotions into creative work. In love, you give your all and long to be fulfilled, but often end up giving yourself to unworthy lovers.

OCTOBER 8

You're expressive and thoroughly likeable, and have an easy way with people. Mostly, your intensity is a secret; it comes out only in intimate relationships. There you struggle for control, yet you want to be open and uninhibited—a difficult balancing act.

OCTOBER 9

You're a coolheaded charmer who underneath is very passionate. Your combination of lightness and seriousness makes the work you do appealing to the public and gives people food for thought. In love, you want to fall head-over-heels and also to communicate.

OCTOBER 10

The flamboyant, risk-taking part of you does coexist with the you who wants safety and security, but this dichotomy makes you feel like two different people. You need a mate who will nourish and understand you. After trial and error, you're promised this.

OCTOBER 11

You're a warrior with the soul of a poet. You're both practical and intuitive; you think things over carefully then make up your mind with your heart. Though you seem aloof, you're sensual and deeply loving. Relationships are your arena for spiritual lessons.

OCTOBER 12

Your innovative mind and passionate spirit are your core. They see you through many adventures—and struggles. You're a real romantic, although you tend to be domineering. Still, you're learning that when you keep your palm open, the sand doesn't run through.

OCTOBER 13

You have common sense (a rare quality), and your intelligent mind works so fast you sometimes neglect your day-to-day chores. Hidden deep within you is a romantic streak. In a relationship, you try to create magic and tend to spoil a lover with attention.

OCTOBER 14

You yearn for excitement, more knowledge, and to live a passionate life. You're known as a "character," and your work will always have an unconventional edge. Love is very important, though you'd rather be alone than be under someone's control.

OCTOBER 15

You're quick-thinking and have people-talent, and your great strength is your receptive mind. Money cheers you up, and you're smart about business. Your flirtatious eye has gotten you into trouble, but when you fall in love, you're true blue.

OCTOBER 16

Despite being highly motivated, you're the soul of cooperation. Indeed, luck follows you in partnerships, and people respond to your fresh, open spontaneity. In love, you're passionate and quick to express your feelings, and you can become quite possessive.

OCTOBER 17

You're a mystic and deep thinker, but you show a jovial face to the world. Others don't know how complicated you are. You have a theatrical quality that can gain a lucrative income. Romantically, you're charismatic, and need to choose someone remarkable.

OCTOBER 18

Restless and full of initiative, you have a daredevil quality others envy. Though you may feel burdened and cooped up, you are in fact a free spirit with one-of-a-kind talents. In love, be careful not to settle for someone less intelligent than you.

OCTOBER 19

You're a wanderer, certainly emotionally if not physically. You're on a quest—to find love, self-expression, fulfillment, understanding from others. You have amazing creative gifts. Being in an intimate relationship brings out your passion and loyalty.

OCTOBER 20

You have undeniable allure, but you try not to get enmeshed in the expectations of those who flock around you. You want freedom to do your thing, especially creatively. Sexually, you seek wildly passionate experiences, though reality often disappoints.

OCTOBER 21

You're enticing, magnetic, with luminous star quality. You combine formidable intelligence with a calm, genial demeanor. You're also a bit of maverick, an out-of-the-box thinker who goes your own way. Sexually, you're intense and like to dominate psychologically.

OCTOBER 22

You have charisma, elegance, and an understanding heart. This makes you a magnet to the public, especially in work in which you interact one-on-one. Love may be your Achilles heel, for you become overprotective and very vulnerable.

YOU AND CHINESE ASTROLOGY

With Marco Polo's adventurous travels in A.D. 1275, Europeans learned for the first time of the great beauty, wealth, history, and romance of China. Untouched as they were by outside influences, the Chinese developed their astrology along different lines from other ancient cultures, such as the Egyptians, Babylonians, and Greeks from whom Western astrology has its roots. Therefore, the Chinese zodiac differs from the zodiac of the West. To begin with, it's based on a lunar cycle rather than Western astrology's solar cycle. The Chinese zodiac is divided into twelve years, and each year is represented by a different animal—the rat, ox, tiger, rabbit, dragon, snake, horse, goat, monkey, rooster, dog, and boar. The legend of the twelve animals is that when Buddha lay on his deathbed, he asked the animals of the forest to come and bid him farewell. These twelve were the first to arrive. The cat, as the story goes, is not among the animals because it was napping and couldn't be bothered to make the journey. (In some Asian countries, however, such as Vietnam, the cat replaces the rabbit.)

Like Western astrology, in which the zodiac signs have different characteristics, each of the twelve Chinese animal years assigns character traits specific to a person born in that year. For example, the Year of the Rat confers honesty and an analytical mind, whereas the Year of the Monkey grants charm and quick ability to spot opportunity.

Here are descriptions for Libra for each Chinese animal year:

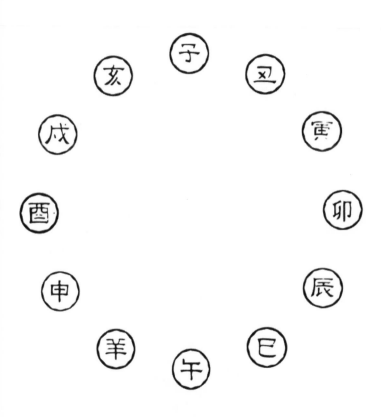

IF YOU ARE LIBRA BORN IN THE YEAR OF THE RAT ⊙

Years of the Rat

1900	1960	2020	2080
1912	1972	2032	2092
1924	1984	2044	
1936	1996	2056	
1948	2008	2068	

In the West, rats are thought of as mean and dirty, but in the Chinese zodiac the Rat is at the head of the line—an imaginative, creative superstar. Rat natives are said to be jolly, sociable, and seductive, as well as highly intelligent—qualities that blend beautifully with your Libran charm and charisma. As a Libran Rat, you're born to be famous in some way. You stand out from the ordinary. You glow from within, a luminescence springing from a strong ambitious streak blended with a gift for making others feel important. Some think you meddle too much and are too acquisitive (you do love beautiful things); it's true your Libran self-absorption is accentuated. Yet you have irresistible *likeability*. In romantic affairs, you make an unforgettable emotional impact; in turn, you do require lots of sensual affection. Compatible partners are born in the Years of the Monkey, Pig, Rat, and Snake.

IF YOU ARE LIBRA BORN IN THE YEAR OF THE OX ⊗

Years of the Ox

1901	1961	2021	2081
1913	1973	2033	2093
1925	1985	2045	
1937	1997	2057	
1949	2009	2069	

One thinks of the ox as lumbering and dull, but in Asia the Ox is revered for its integrity and strength of purpose. Plus it has something more—flair and an ability to please an audience. The Ox has magical significance because of its association with agricultural growth, and an Ox person is said to be a great initiator and leader. This combined with your Libran magnetism gives you eloquence and makes you fascinating to the public. As a Libran Ox, you're highly intelligent, have elegant manners, know how to keep secrets, and are exceedingly stubborn about what you believe is right. You can also be pig-headed and hold grudges, but you're destined to create lasting work. In love, you're passionate and sensual, with deep reserves of romanticism, yet your self-sacrificing ways can cause you heartache. Compatible partners are born in the Years of the Rabbit, Rooster, Monkey, Pig, and Snake.

IF YOU ARE LIBRA BORN IN THE YEAR OF THE TIGER

Years of the Tiger

1902	1962	2022	2082
1914	1974	2034	2094
1926	1986	2046	
1938	1998	2058	
1950	2010	2070	

The Chinese Tiger symbolizes the power of faith, and this quality infuses the Year of the Tiger with strength of purpose and a valorous spirit. Chinese believe a Tiger year brings overthrow of the old—and Tiger passion and pride blend with your Libran allure to create a stand-out rebel. You may cloak your "noncompliance" in charming manners, yet you'll always be a revolutionary who makes your own rules. You certainly understand commitment and hard work, but you go your own way to pursue your destiny of an unusual life. You have great style; people copy your taste in dress and decoration. In a career, you're driven by a need to win (your dreams and goals), and in love you display this same urge to possess and dominate. But you have a wandering eye, and it may take a long time to find true peace of heart. Compatible partners are born in the Years of the Rabbit, Dog, Dragon, Monkey, Tiger, and Pig.

IF YOU ARE LIBRA BORN IN THE YEAR OF THE RABBIT

Years of the Rabbit

1903	1963	2023	2083
1915	1975	2035	2095
1927	1987	2047	
1939	1999	2059	
1951	2011	2071	

The Year of the Rabbit (or, in countries such as Vietnam, the Cat), endows its natives with charm, curiosity, and ambition. These characteristics are already very Libran and heighten your pronounced ability to captivate. As a Libran Rabbit, you're talkative, theatrical, powerfully seductive, and richly imaginative. A born communicator, you're particularly good at work that requires diplomacy. You're also blessed with a gift for choosing endeavors that make money. However, even more than financial security you want to live an adventurous, *fabulous* life. Some may say you're superficial, but this is because you won't be swayed to think as they do. The one you do bend over backward to please is a lover. You're delightfully sexual but also exhibit a flirtatiousness that arouses jealousy. Compatible partners are born in the Years of the Goat, Dog, Dragon, Snake, Horse, and Monkey.

IF YOU ARE LIBRA BORN IN THE YEAR OF THE DRAGON

Years of the Dragon

1904	1964	2024	2084
1916	1976	2036	2096
1928	1988	2048	
1940	2000	2060	
1952	2012	2072	

In Asian mythology, the Dragon is the guardian of treasure. It represents royalty, wisdom, power, and the spirit of change. Born in the Year of the Dragon, you are chosen for a special destiny—to choose unusual paths and complicated emotional scenarios. The Dragon fearlessness counteracts any Libran reticence and magnifies your ability to connect to people who promote your talents. You have flash, enthusiasm, and extraordinary pluck, and you know that life gives you exactly what you put into it. True, you're prone to procrastination and much self-indulgence; you're also stubborn and rigid. But when you take action, you're a powerhouse. You're a great lover, sensual and seductive, and have a profound effect on your partners' lives. You can be intense and prone to jealousy, yet you also need a lot of space. Compatible partners are born in the Years of the Rabbit, Goat, Monkey, Snake, and Tiger.

IF YOU ARE LIBRA BORN IN THE YEAR OF THE SNAKE

Years of the Snake

1905	1965	2025	2085
1917	1977	2037	2097
1929	1989	2049	
1941	2001	2061	
1953	2013	2073	

The Chinese Snake is elegant, eloquent, and filled with humor. Contrary to the West's snake of cold-bloodedness, in Asia the Snake is the Goddess of Beauty and the Sea, associated with romance and art. Snake intuition and intelligence add to Libra's ability to read others, and the Libran Snake is a hit with the public. You're used to having people fall at your feet, yet you're not arrogant. Indeed, your egalitarian spirit and sense of fun contribute mightily to your career success. Mainly you're a sage who loves knowledge, and you strive to express yourself through creative work. You do enjoy spending other people's money, but are also generous with your own. The Snake represents regeneration, and in love you're a sensitive, sensual nurturer. Your love affairs are often about healing old pain and creating new life. Compatible partners are born in the Years of the Rabbit, Rooster, Dragon, Horse, Ox, and Rat.

IF YOU ARE LIBRA BORN IN THE YEAR OF THE HORSE

Years of the Horse

1906	1966	2026	2086
1918	1978	2038	2098
1930	1990	2050	
1942	2002	2062	
1954	2014	2074	

The Horse has extraordinary power. In China a Horse year is so significant that pregnancies are planned around giving birth at this time. The Horse signifies heroism, leadership, and exploration—and being born in the Year of the Horse speaks of achieving some kind of fame. Horse fervor and persuasion strengthen your Libran ambition. You have a fertile imagination and a vivid personality, and you enjoy popularity with an audience. As a Libran Horse, you're rebellious, but you channel this into being a true original and saying yes to new ventures. You're built for hard work, though of course the work must be your *own* choosing; you're not an invisible drone. In romantic affairs, you're a passionate, head-over-heels lover, but you need a partner as intelligent and vibrantly emotional as you to keep your interest engaged. Compatible partners are born in the Years of the Rabbit, Rooster, Goat, Horse, and Snake.

IF YOU ARE LIBRA BORN IN THE YEAR OF THE GOAT

Years of the Goat

1907	1967	2027	2087
1919	1979	2039	2099
1931	1991	2051	
1943	2003	2063	
1955	2015	2075	

In the West, the goat has a lascivious connotation, but the Asian Goat is supremely artistic and inventive, filled with knowledge, and considered a messenger of the gods. The Year of the Goat confers idealism that makes your Libran sweetness even more radiant. Along with social grace, you have a charming bohemian quality, a way of bounding off into unusual byways and pursuing your non-conformist interests. Inquisitive and a voracious seeker of knowledge, you look for truth. You want to do work that expresses the real you and be honest in relationships. Yes, you can be undisciplined and capricious, and at times exhibit a "not there" detachment, but you're sincere. Love is your arena for lessons. A schemer can take advantage of your trusting nature, yet ultimately you're promised an amazing relationship with a soulmate. Compatible partners are born in the Years of the Rabbit, Dragon, Horse, Monkey, and Pig.

IF YOU ARE LIBRA BORN IN THE YEAR OF THE MONKEY

⊕

Years of the Monkey

1908	1968	2028	2088
1920	1980	2040	2100
1932	1992	2052	
1944	2004	2064	
1956	2016	2076	

The Chinese Monkey is witty, playful, and intelligent. In Asian mythology, the Monkey is the vivacious companion of the God of Sailors, and this effervescence is gifted to you born in the Year of the Monkey. Indeed, Monkey cleverness and allure increase your Libra people-skills to create a personality lit with charisma. Primarily, you're an actor who can cover your feelings and fit yourself to the occasion. Thus, you're brilliant at dealing with large groups and snatching opportunity. Endowed with curiosity and a remarkable memory, you have a freewheeling air others find charming; they seem to forgive the fact you tend to bend the truth. You know how to enchant, never more so than in the romantic arena. For you, the best part is falling in love and the hardest staying in love. Sexually, you're amazingly inventive. Compatible partners are born in the Years of the Rabbit, Dragon, Ox, Pig, Rat, and Tiger.

IF YOU ARE LIBRA BORN IN THE YEAR OF THE ROOSTER

Years of the Rooster

1909	1957	2005	2053
1921	1969	2017	2065
1933	1981	2029	2077
1945	1993	2041	2089

The Chinese Rooster symbolizes courage and, in Asian mythology, is the one who rescues the Goddess of the Sun. The Year of the Rooster confers an adventurous spirit, unique talents, and a life of achievement. Rooster resourcefulness enhances your Libran creativity, making you daring in presenting yourself to people and known for your one-of-a-kind work. Indeed, you have the reputation of being a bit eccentric, but this is because you're completely outspoken. (People have trouble with the truth.) You love novelty, are independent, and have a resilience that bounces back from reverses. Though you give off an assured, devil-may-care attitude (possibly because you tend to be a spendthrift), in fact you're highly responsible. This is especially true in love, where you look for long-term commitment. You must be careful not to become the one who does all the sacrificing. Compatible partners are born in the Years of the Horse, Ox, and Snake.

IF YOU ARE LIBRA BORN IN THE YEAR OF THE DOG

Years of the Dog

1910	1958	2006	2054
1922	1970	2018	2066
1934	1982	2030	2078
1946	1994	2042	2090

Like its real-life counterpart, the Asian Dog is faithful and protective. The Chinese believe those born in the Year of the Dog display the best traits in human nature—honesty, compassion, kindness, and trustworthiness. Dog commitment and foresight blend seamlessly with your Libran intelligence and intuitive understanding of people. The result is you have assertiveness (which many Librans lack) and willingness to forge ahead. You also have a shrewd head for making money, which is all to the good because you love to spend it. People know you can be counted on to keep your promises. What you hide is that you're a worrier, and you do try to control situations so nothing goes wrong. Love brings out your fiercest loyalty, and you can be downright selfless. You are a faultfinder, however, and sometimes too exacting in what you demand from a lover. Compatible partners are born in the Years of the Cat, Dog, Pig, and Tiger.

IF YOU ARE LIBRA BORN IN THE YEAR OF THE PIG

Years of the Pig

1911	1959	2007	2055
1923	1971	2019	2067
1935	1983	2031	2079
1947	1995	2043	2091

In the West, the pig is held in low regard, but in China the Pig is a noble creature—gallant, chivalrous, scrupulous, and heroic. Being born in the Year of the Pig is said to bring great honor, for you're an intellectual and a tastemaker. Indeed, Pig strength, warmth, elegance, and love for the finer things of life underline your Libran aesthetics. As a Libran Pig, you can create a rich existence—not only monetary riches but a cultured mind and superb sense of style. In a career, you have a touch for putting a new spin on the old (e.g., in the fields of antiques, anthropology, history). Relationships are your métier, for nothing is more important than maintaining close bonds and emotional equilibrium. In love, you are deeply romantic and sexually lavish. Yet you must choose carefully; you can be victimized by your naïveté. Compatible partners are born in the Years of the Rabbit, Dog, Pig, and Tiger.

YOU AND NUMEROLOGY

Numerology is the language of numbers. It is the belief that there is a correlation between numbers and living things, ideas, and concepts. Certainly, numbers surround and infuse our lives (e.g., twenty-four hours in a day, twelve months of the year, etc.). And from ancient times mystics have taught that numbers carry a *vibration*, a deeper meaning that defines how each of us fits into the universe. According to numerology, you are born with a personal number that contains information about who you are and what you need to be happy. This number expresses what numerology calls your life path.

All numbers reduce to one of nine digits, numbers 1 through 9. Your personal number is based on your date of birth. To calculate your number, write your birth date in numerals. As an example, the birth date of September 25, 1984, is written 9-25-1984. Now begin the addition: 9 + 25 + 1 + 9 + 8 + 4 = 56; 56 reduces to 5 + 6 = 11; 11 reduces to 1 + 1 = 2. The personal number for someone born September 25, 1984, is *Two*.

IF YOU ARE A LIBRA ONE

Keywords: Confidence and Creativity

One is the number of leadership and new beginnings. You rush into whatever engages your heart—whether a new plan, a love affair, or just finding more pleasure. You're courageous and inventive, and attracted to unusual creative pursuits because you like to be one-of-a-kind. Your contagious warmth draws others to you, but you also need your space. You can't bear to be under the thumb of other people's whims and agendas. Careers that call to you are those in which you are in charge and able to work independently. As for love, you want ecstasy and passion, and the most exciting part of a flirtation is the beginning.

IF YOU ARE A LIBRA TWO

Keywords: Cooperation and Balance

Two is the number of cooperation and creating a secure entity. Being a Two underlines your Libran magnetism—you attract what you need. Your magic is not only your people skills, but your ability to breathe life into empty forms (e.g., a concept, an ambitious business idea, a new relationship) and produce something of worth. In your work, you're a perfectionist—and because you have both a creative side *and* a practical side, you're drawn to careers that combine a business sense with an artistic challenge. In love, your deepest desire is for a loving partnership with someone you can trust and share confidences with.

IF YOU ARE A LIBRA THREE

Keywords: Expression and Sensitivity

Three symbolizes self-expression. You have a gift for words and a talent for visualization. Three is the number of the "connector." You link people together so that they benefit from each other. You stimulate others to think. In career, Libran creativity and innovation are your specialties. You're a quick study, mentally active, and are curious about the new (though you tend to be distractible). In love, you need someone who excites you intellectually and sensually, and understands your complex personality. Casual acquaintances may not see your depth, but in love you must have a soulmate who does.

IF YOU ARE A LIBRA FOUR

Keywords: Stability and Process

Four is the number of dedication and loyalty. It represents *foundation*, exactly as a four-sided square does. Being a Four underlines your need for security. You are a builder, and the direction you go in is up. First you plan, then day-by-day you add the next step. You create stability by following a process, and your strength is that you're persistent. Therefore, you're able to accomplish great works. Your spiritual quest is to discover self worth. In love, you look for a relationship with staying power. You need a faithful, giving, and understanding lover with whom you can express your rich sensuality.

IF YOU ARE A LIBRA FIVE

Keywords: Freedom and Discipline

Five is the number of change and freedom. With your chameleon intellect (it can go in any direction) and captivating ability to deal with people, you're a marvelous *persuader*. You charm and influence others, and have great skill with the public. As a Five, you're a Libran very capable of utilizing your ability to initiate. In your work you don't become stuck, and you know how to let go of the unfeasible. In love, you need romantic fantasy but also want a partner who looks ahead to new goals. When you give your heart away it's to someone with whom you passionately mesh—body and mind.

IF YOU ARE A LIBRA SIX

Keywords: Vision and Acceptance

Six is the number of teaching, healing, and utilizing your talents. You're geared toward changing the world or at least fixing other people's lives. Being an advice-giver and even a therapist to your friends comes naturally. Love really does rule your universe, but your life is not just sweetness and light. You can be exacting and demanding—especially with yourself. You're your own harshest critic, for you hold yourself up to a standard of excellence and secretly don't feel worthy enough. In love, you're fervent about being a helpmate and confidante. You're also a sensualist who gives your all to someone you trust.

IF YOU ARE A LIBRA SEVEN

Keywords: Trust and Openness

Seven is the number of the mystic and the intensely focused specialist. You're an intriguing "inner workings" person—you see into human nature and in a flash understand how things work (in business, in relationships). You're an intellectual, a philosopher, and a connoisseur of everything creative. Your heart's desire is to surround yourself with things of value—a loving mate, family, creative work, authentic relationships. Romantically, you attract many but choose few. At your core you're extremely loyal and intensely loving, and your deepest need is for a partner who can help you in your journey to becoming the real you.

IF YOU ARE A LIBRA EIGHT

Keywords: Abundance and Power

Eight is the number of mastery and authority. You are intelligent, alert, quick in action, and more decisive than many Librans. You work well in large groups because you see what's needed and know how to maneuver. Eight opens a path to material gain, which of course you enjoy, but your real passion is to prove yourself and do well in your *own* eyes. You enjoy reaching out to diversified groups, traveling, adding to your education, being in the limelight. In love, giving your commitment is a serious act. You are a protective and deeply caring lover, and in turn you need to know your lover is your unwavering ally.

IF YOU ARE A LIBRA NINE

Keywords: Integrity and Wisdom

Nine is the path of the "old soul," the number of completion and full bloom. Because it's the last number, it sums up the highs and lows of human experience, and you live a life of dramatic events. You're intellectual, deeply feeling, extremely protective, interested in all kinds of exploration. People see you as colorful and heroic because you have an expansive outlook but are also spiritual and altruistic. In love, you're truthful and sincere—as well as a romantic, highly sensual creature. As a Libra Nine you generously give of yourself, often to the point of being sacrificing.

LAST WORD: YOUR LIBRA UNFINISHED BUSINESS

Psychologists often use the phrase *unfinished business* to describe unresolved issues—for example, patterns from childhood that cause unhappiness, anger that keeps one stuck, scenarios of family dysfunction that repeat through second and third generations (such as alcoholism or abusive behavior).

Astrology teaches that the past is indeed very much with us in the present—and that using astrological insights can help us to move out of emotional darkness into greater clarity. Even within this book (which is not a tome of hundreds of pages) you have read of many of the superlatives and challenges of being Libra. You have breathtaking gifts and at the same time certain tendencies that can undermine utilizing these abilities.

In nature, a fascinating fact is that in jungles and forests a poisonous plant will grow in a certain spot and always, just a few feet away, is a plant that is the antidote to that specific poison. Likewise, in astrology, the antidote is right there ready to be used when the negatives threaten to overwhelm your life.

Libra's unfinished business has to do with your nagging sense of being deficient. Astrologically, the Sun (which represents the ego) is weak in the sign of Libra—whereas it is strong in Aries, your zodiacal opposite. You have great difficulty enjoying and being thankful for your extraordinary gifts—gifts anyone else would envy. Your critical inner voice tells you others are better, smarter, stronger than you and that you need others to take care of you.

Of course, all this is enclosed in a dark interior corner, and obviously you do function brilliantly in the outside world. You're brainy, talented, superior at dealing with people. Yet you pull a heavy cart behind you, filled with brooding questions such as "Am I all right?" "Am I smart enough to understand this?" "Do I look fat?" "Is that person cold to me?" "What have I done not to be liked?"

You have superior intelligence, yet you often use your mind to make your life more difficult. You whirl around in your head, sifting through negative thoughts, hurts, resentment, indecision, and confusion. You dwell on your second-guessings and insecurities.

Libra is the sign of balance, which doesn't mean you arrive in this life fully balanced—it means you search for balance. You need to fight your tendency to tip from one end of the scale to the other. You feel joyous highs, and in a while you're down. Up and down, like a seesaw.

Libra is also the sign of relationships, and, being other-oriented, you project on others what you want in yourself. You see a partner, lover, boss, colleague as competent, talented, wise, having sound judgment. You assign power to the other rather than to yourself.

You ruminate about small crises. As a communicator, you want to talk and discuss and arrive at an answer as to why these crises continually happen to you. If you could hear yourself, it would be clear that though the scenario changes, the essential story remains the same. Others have taken advantage of your sweetness and willingness to give, and you can't understand why. You fail to see, by and large, it's you yourself who initiate the crises because of your own sense of insecurity.

All this sounds as if you're a basket case, which is certainly untrue! Your emotional roiling around takes place subterraneanly—but it does take place, and these fears and struggles undermine your happiness. They stand in the way of your embracing your wonderful self as *wonderful*.

Yet the antidotes are there to be found in their entirety in being Libra, for you are indeed shining, brilliant, successful, possessing magical talents. You're exceedingly smart, and no one has your skill with people. Your head is filled with knowledge and your heart with abundant generosity.

Because your mind is powerful, your thoughts shape your reality. *You* are what you think; it's your belief that's real to you. Yet you can learn to control your negative thoughts. You can literally talk to your negative thoughts the way you would talk to a negative person. By consciously focusing on your strengths, you can learn self-love, compassion, and kindness for *yourself*. You can take responsibility for you.

This is not an overnight process; it takes discipline, patience, and persistence. But you have everything you need in your Libran arsenal to access your incredible power of self.

FAMOUS PEOPLE WITH THE SUN IN LIBRA

Julie Andrews
Hannah Arendt
Armand Assante
Brigitte Bardot
David Ben-Gurion
Joyce Brothers
Art Buchwald
Truman Capote
Al Capp
Miguel de Cervantes
Ray Charles
Montgomery Clift
Jackie Collins
Simon Cowell
e. e. cummings
Matt Damon
Catherine Deneuve
Angie Dickinson
Michael Douglas
William O. Douglas
Alfred Drake
Hilary Duff
Eleanor Duse
Dwight D. Eisenhower
Britt Ekland
T. S. Eliot
William Faulkner
Carrie Fisher
F. Scott Fitzgerald
Annette Funicello
John Kenneth Galbraith
Mohandas K. Gandhi
George Gershwin
Bryant Gumbel
Linda Hamilton

Helen Hayes
Rita Hayworth
Jim Henson
Vladimir Horowitz
Lee Iacocca
Julio Iglesias
Jesse Jackson
Donna Karan
Buster Keaton
Deborah Kerr
Evel Knievel
Angela Lansbury
Ralph Lauren
John LeCarré
Ursula K. LeGuin
John Lennon
Walter Lippmann
Carole Lombard
Yo-Yo Ma
Mickey Mantle
Wynton Marsalis
Groucho Marx
Marcello Mastroianni
Johnny Mathis
Walter Matthau
John Mayer
Mark McGwire
Melina Mercouri
Arthur Miller
Yves Montand
Martina Navratilova
Admiral Horatio Nelson
Louise Nevelson
Eugene O'Neill
Gwenyth Paltrow

Luciano Pavarotti
Juan Perón
Luke Perry
Paul Potts
Mario Puzo
Christopher Reeve
Anne Rice
Kelly Ripa
Rex Reed
Tim Robbins
Mickey Rooney
Eleanor Roosevelt
Susan Sarandon
George C. Scott
Paul Simon
Ashlee Simpson
Will Smith
Annika Sorenstam
Bruce Springsteen
Gwen Stefani
Wallace Stevens
Sting
Ed Sullivan
Margaret Thatcher
Cheryl Tiegs
Desmond Tutu
Usher
Giuseppe Verdi
Ben Vereen
Gore Vidal
Barbara Walters
Sigourney Weaver
Oscar Wilde
Serena Williams
Thomas Wolfe

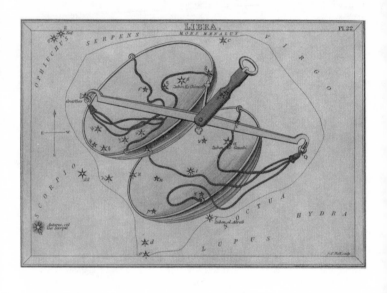

PART TWO

ALL ABOUT YOUR SIGN OF LIBRA

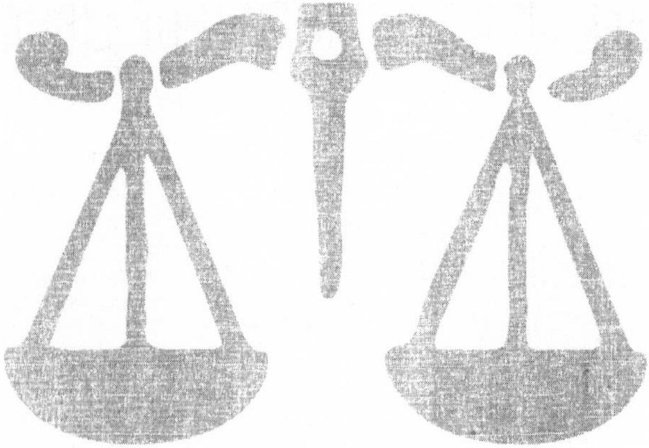

LIBRA'S ASTROLOGICAL AFFINITIES, LINKS, AND LORE

SYMBOL: THE SCALES

Signifying balance, equilibrium, order, and justice. In the ancient world, the balance-scale was an analogy of two halves becoming a perfect whole, and thus symbolizes the joining of female and male, day and night, light and dark. In Egyptian mythology, the Goddess of Justice, Maat, held the scales. In modern times, the image of a woman holding the scales in one hand and the sword of justice in the other is a powerful symbol of our legal system. The Libran Scales of Balance also represent the equinox—the Sun enters Libra on the day of the Autumn Equinox.

RULING PLANET: Venus ♀

Roman goddess of pleasure, beauty, adornment, the arts, love, sensuality, and harmonious relationships. In Latin, the word *Venus* means love and sexual desire. The Roman goddess Venus was the Greek goddess Aphrodite whose dominion was seduction and enticement. Astrologically, Venus's influence also inclines toward a love of luxury, exceptional creative ability, charming sociability, and a bent toward self-indulgence. Venus is linked to the capacity to express affection and enjoy beauty.

DOMINANT KEYWORD

I BALANCE

GLYPH ♎

The pictograph represents the Scales in perfect equilibrium. This was the ancient Egyptian symbol for the setting sun, which was regarded as the doorway between two worlds. In symbolic terms, the glyph is a crescent moon connected to two straight lines resting above a third line. This represents emotion bounded on either side by reason; the line below symbolizes partnership.

PART OF THE BODY RULED BY LIBRA: The Lower Back and Buttocks and the Kidneys

Librans suffer from lower back strain and problems in the lumbar region. They are also subject to kidney infections.

LUCKY DAY: Friday

The day named for Venus, ruler of Libra. Friday comes from the Old English *frigedaeg* (Day of Frige), which was a translation from the Latin for Day of Venus. This day is said to bring passion and harmony into your life.

LUCKY NUMBERS: 6 and 9

Numerologically, 6 is the number of relationships and the balance of opposites—and 9 is linked to completion and limitless understanding. These themes align with the nature of Libra.

TAROT CARD: Justice

The card in the Tarot linked to Libra is Justice. Ancient names for the Justice card are Daughter of the Lords of Truth and Ruler of the Balance. In the Tarot, this card signifies balance and well-deliberated judgment. It speaks of a wise verdict based on careful consideration. Justice points to the need to stay fair and remain incorruptible, and to seek equilibrium between opposing forces in your life. When this card turns up in a Tarot reading, it says you will reap what you sow and that you are responsible for the end result.

The card itself pictures the female figure of Justice seated between two pillars. Her right hand holds a sword, and her left a balance-scale. The sword cuts through to the truth, and the scale represents a balanced decision. The pillars symbolize positive and negative, and Justice sits in equilibrium between them. She is not blindfolded; her eyes are wide open to see with great clarity.

For Libra, Justice tells you that when you are balanced within yourself, you can find integrity, courage, and the capacity to love. You will make the right decision in all things.

MAGICAL BIRTHSTONE: Opal

A gemstone of ever-changing iridescent colors reflecting the splendor of nature (the Sun, fire, the rainbow, oceans, mountains, and trees). The opal's internal structure diffracts light and takes on many colors—and in Australia, where most opals are mined, the mythology is that the gods came down in a rainbow to bring peace to human beings. The stone itself retains a high degree of water (often more than 10 percent of its mass), making it sensitive to temperature changes; thus the opal is said to bestow sensitivity. The "fire" in the opal symbolizes an eye, which gives the gem its protective powers. The stone is also thought to confer psychic vision. For Librans, the opal is said to free you from jealousy and greed, dispel depression, bring financial success, and help to find true love.

SPECIAL COLORS: Blue and Lavender

The colors of romance, harmony, peace, and refinement. Blue is particularly linked to truth and intellect, and lavender to peace and spirituality.

CONSTELLATION OF LIBRA

Libra was once part of the constellation of Virgo, and later part of the constellation Scorpio. Libra, the Latin name for "weighing scales," is the most modern of the twelve constellations of the zodiac, the last to be named, and the only one that does not represent a living creature. In early Mesopotamia, the Libra star-grouping was called both a Scale and the Claws of the Scorpion because the weighing scale of that era resembled a scorpion hung up by the end of its tail with its arms stretched out. In Greek mythology, Libra is the scales held by Astraea, the Virgo goddess of justice. From antiquity the constellation of Libra has represented the equinox and the concept of balance, justice, and the weighing of goods and issues.

CITIES

Vienna, Copenhagen, Charleston, Lisbon

COUNTRIES

Burma, China, Tibet, Japan, Argentina

FLOWERS

Rose, Cosmos, and Hydrangea

TREES

Almond, Cypress, and Ash

HERBS AND SPICES

Mint, Arrack, and Cayenne

METAL: Copper

A malleable metal prized for its beautiful color and thermal conductivity. Copper has been in use for over ten thousand years. This metal was sacred to the goddess Venus, and the written symbol for copper and for the planet Venus (ruler of Libra) is the same. In the ancient world, copper that was fashioned into lightning rods was used as protection against lightning, and therefore considered a guard against all evil influences. Egyptians placed copper behind the heads of mummies to provide "warmth" on their journey to the afterlife. Copper is also thought to have healing powers; even today copper bracelets are worn as an antidote to the aches and pains of arthritis and rheumatism.

ANIMALS RULED BY LIBRA

Snakes and Lizards

DANGER

Libra people tend to stir up ill feelings from others in situations having to do with love. Because they are indecisive and some-times make a declaration of love too easily, Librans both anger and disappoint lovers. They also have a tendency to be fickle and faithless.

PERSONAL PROVERBS

Shared joy is a double joy; shared sorrow is half a sorrow.

Keep a green tree in your heart and perhaps a singing bird will come.

KEYWORDS FOR LIBRA

Sociable
Artistic
Attractive
Sophisticated
Diplomatic
Gracious
Popular
Seductive
Sensual
Sensitive

Cooperative
Adaptive
Compliant
Team worker
Procrastinating
Indecisive
Self-doubting
Ambivalent
Narcissistic
Subtle
Manipulative
Self-indulgent
Rational
Detached
Multiple relationships
Paradoxical

HOW ASTROLOGY SLICES AND DICES YOUR SIGN OF LIBRA

DUALITY: Masculine

The twelve astrological signs are divided into two groups, *masculine* and *feminine*. Six are masculine and six are feminine; this is known as the sign's *duality*. A masculine sign is direct and energetic. A feminine sign is receptive and magnetic. These attributes were given to the signs about 2,500 years ago. Today modern astrologers avoid the sexism implicit in these distinctions. A masculine sign does not mean "positive and forceful" any more than a feminine sign means "negative and weak." In modern terminology, the masculine signs, such as your sign of Libra, are defined as outer-directed and strong through action. The feminine signs are self-contained and strong through inner reserves.

TRIPLICITY (ELEMENT): Air

The twelve signs are also divided into groups of three signs each. These three-sign groups are called a *triplicity*, and each of these denotes an *element*. The elements are *Fire*, *Earth*, *Air*, and *Water*. In astrology, an element symbolizes a fundamental characterization of the sign.

The three *Fire* signs are Aries, Leo, and Sagittarius. Fire signs are active and enthusiastic.

The three *Earth* signs are Taurus, Virgo, and Capricorn. Earth signs are practical and stable.

The three *Air* signs are Gemini, Libra, and Aquarius. Air signs are intellectual and communicative.

The three *Water* signs are Cancer, Scorpio, and Pisces. Water signs are emotional and intuitive.

QUADRUPLICITY (QUALITY): Cardinal

The twelve signs are also divided into groups of four signs each. These four-sign groups are called a *quadruplicity*, and each of these denotes a *quality*. The qualities are *Cardinal*, *Fixed*, and *Mutable*. In astrology, the quality signifies the sign's interaction with the outside world.

Four signs are *Cardinal** signs. They are Aries, Cancer, Libra, and Capricorn. Cardinal signs are enterprising and outgoing. They are the initiators and leaders.

*When the Sun crosses the four cardinal points in the zodiac, we mark the beginning of each of our four seasons. Aries begins spring; Cancer begins summer; Libra begins fall; Capricorn begins winter.

Four signs are *Fixed*. They are Taurus, Leo, Scorpio, and Aquarius. Fixed signs are resistant to change. They hold on; they're perfecters and finishers, rather than originators.

Four signs are *Mutable*. They are Gemini, Virgo, Sagittarius, and Pisces. Mutable signs are flexible, versatile, and adaptable. They are able to adjust to differing circumstances.

Your sign of Libra is a Masculine, Air, Cardinal sign—and no other sign in the zodiac is this exact combination. Your sign is a one-of-a-kind combination, and therefore you express the characteristics of your duality, element, and quality differently from any other sign.

For example, your sign is a *Masculine* sign, meaning you are active, outgoing, ambitious. You're an *Air* sign, meaning you're intelligent, highly expressive, and fascinated with ideas. And you're a *Cardinal* sign, meaning you're enterprising, an initiator and creator, able to embark on the new.

Now, the sign of Gemini is also Masculine and Air, but unlike Libra (which is Cardinal), Gemini is Mutable. Like you, Gemini is energetic, intelligent, gifted at directing others, highly social, and communicative. Both Libra and Gemini radiate charm and are highly social. But Gemini is easily distracted, changeable: It tends to take on too many projects and commitments, and to scatter its energy. Gemini doesn't have your ability to make the first move and then follow through. One of Gemini's fears is confinement, and its mutability shows up as a tendency to flee from situations and relationships that feel restrictive. You, being Cardinal, are definitely an activist who will set out on an independent path and stay on it to reach your goal. The Libran Cardinal quality is also evident in your dynamic ability to initiate relationships (professionally and personally) and fill them with your energy.

Aquarius, too, is Masculine and Air, but unlike Libra (which is Cardinal), Aquarius is Fixed. Aquarius, like you, has great intellectual curiosity, is charming, friendly, and very oriented toward others. You both have in common a love of ideas. However, being Fixed, Aquarius is stubborn about its ideas, unbending in its opinions, and unwilling to admit a mistake. Aquarius is deeply invested what it *thinks*, and to back down from a viewpoint feels like a betrayal of self. Aquarians describe themselves as persistent, but in truth they are resistant. You, being Cardinal, are open to new ways of thinking and very fond of looking at all possibilities. Libra is willing to scrap an unworkable plan and start in another direction. You won't get so stuck on a pet notion that it stops you from getting a *result* you want.

POLARITY: Aries

The twelve signs are also divided into groups of two signs each. These two-sign groups are called a *polarity* (meaning "opposite"). Each sign in the zodiac has a polarity, which is its opposite sign in the other half of the zodiac. The two signs express opposite characteristics.

Libra and Aries are a polarity. Libra is the sign of partnership, marriage, legal unions and agreements, and joining into a bond. It signifies the principle of balance and harmony. You are happiest when combining with others, being in close personal and professional relationships, and generating cooperation. You have an instinct for drawing people together and being a mediator and peacemaker. Libra is always aware of the subtle ways in which people and things relate—and its energies go into maintaining equilibrium. Libra also symbolizes artistry and refined aesthetics, and you're known for your gift for bringing beauty into the world.

Aries, your opposite sign, is the sign of ego, personality, and self. Aries people tend to put themselves first and assert their own will. Aries is anything but hesitant—it rushes ahead at breakneck speed to get to its goal. Archetypically, Aries is the conquering warrior who goes forward with courage. What drives Aries is egocentricity—the ego at the center. As the first sign of the zodiac, Aries's motivation is to develop *self* and to imprint that self on the world. Ariens are far more interested in projecting themselves into the spotlight than becoming the equal half of a partnership.

Astrologically, you as a Libran can benefit from adopting some of Aries assertiveness and willingness to set out alone. Libra can get very dependent on being liked. You push down your real feelings and keep trying to please. Aries will go its own way and find wonderful experiences in the process. Defeat doesn't stop Aries for long; its optimism, boldness, and confidence propel it forward. Tapping into these qualities would serve you well, Libra. You can be hesitant, fearful of rejection or failure. In addition, you tend to hold back while you ponder, trying to make a perfect decision (and there are no perfect decisions). By taking on some Aries boldness, you will spare yourself angst and suffering. As the expression goes, *Just Do It!*—and you can open far more exciting life adventures.

In turn, Aries has much to learn from you. Among the most important is the strength derived from being deeply linked to others. Connections create a web of support. Having a singular point of view (one's self) blocks the vision outward. Aries lacks understanding of others because it doesn't truly see others. Psychologically, Aries is the selfish baby who never gets past the "me" stage.

Aries has a way of hurting people through thoughtlessness and in-consideration and can certainly learn from Libra's ability to sense how another is reacting. The power to see is one of Libra's great attributes—and Aries can discover from you that seeing beauty and graciousness (instead of competition and strife) makes life joyful. Most of all, Aries can learn that true wisdom of the heart arises out of love and understanding, not conflict and "winning."